Thank you, God, for Thanksgiving, for our family and for our friends. For it is in giving thanks that we truly celebrate your abundant gifts of love and grace.

Printed in the USA

Prayer Garden Press

God Blesses

Us with

Thanksgiving

Evana Vincent

Thank you, God, for the bright colors of autumn along the way and the cool air blowing through the trees.

Once autumn has arrived and leaves are changing to all the bright yellows and oranges, Thanksgiving is here. Winding paths weaving through country hills is God's great splendor.

Now the trees are thinning out their leaves and the air has become quite a chill.

Under the sides of the hills and tucked inside the thicket are numerous bugs, beetles and crickets. "Chirp, thick, thick," says the cricket. "Chirp, thick, thick." Do you see the cricket?

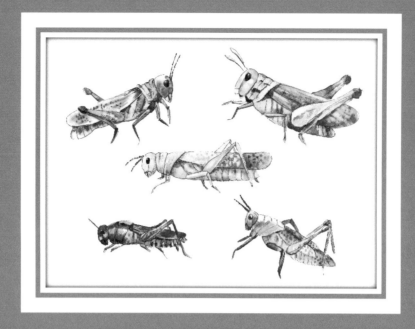

Thank you, God, for the bugs hidden away, under rocks and crickets that chirp and hop. Thank you for all your funny and silly bugs.

Flocks of geese fly in formation to go south for the winter. You can watch as they form lines across the evening sky calling out, "haaaannk, haaaannnnk."

Berries and fruits grow in abundance and the autumn harvest has brought our Thanksgiving feast. "Coo, coo, cheeep, cheeep," sings the red-tipped black bird. "Coo, coo."

"An autumn feast awaits you at the farm," announces Farmer Pfister to his grandkids. "The garden harvest is overflowing! Fill your baskets full and carry them home - as much as you can carry. Let us eat from this bountiful land."

Thank you, God, for the land that grows our fruits, our vegetables and our grains. Thank you for the harvest season that gives us the great reward of our labor.

The hay is bailed and the barns are full of the harvest. Pumpkins stacked in wheelbarrows, corn is piled high, squash by the bushel baskets and sweet potato boxes stacked by the doorway, Farmer Pfister can hardly get by.

From atop a branch in the tallest tree on the farm sits a Peregrine falcon, disguised and hidden behind orange-brown leaves. Looking for prey, looking, waiting and watching all day for something to eat. Maybe a cute mouse, I dare say!

Very low, down below, Mr. Scuttle scurries about in the hedge rummaging for food hidden under umbrella-shaped mushrooms.

Thank you, God, for my family and my friends. I love them so and
I am happy to have them share my days.

"Come now," said Farmer Pfister, "collect your favorite foods into your basket and run along home to give to your mother. She is making a fine Thanksgiving meal alongside your grandmother this day. Don't forget to bring home something for the center of your table! God blesses us with Thanksgiving and makes all things new."

Thank you, God, for the variety of taste and color in this food.
What a feast you have planned for us and each season brings it all
new.

"There is corn, and squash, gourds and pomegranate, pears and apples and pumpkins, too," he said. "Grapes, cranberries, potatoes, and spinach if you have more room in there. We can lay more on top. Tuck this one under your arm and try to carry this, too."

Thank you, God, for the gathering and for giving us love here, too. We count all the blessings that come from You and our greatest blessing is You.

The roasted turkey on the center plate, is surrounded by the harvest God gave us. Potatoes, apples, pear and squash, green beans are here, too. The pumpkins from the patch are on the front porch waiting to be eaten. There is every kind of pie to choose from now-- Thanksgiving blessings abound!

Now you can create a centerpiece or any other creative project you would like. You may also cut these out and decorate your Thanksgiving table making place cards, chair decorations or food buffet cards. Ask your parents for safe scissors, tape and glue. Cut along the dotted lines to remove pages from your storybook.

Artist Credit & Recognition

I gratefully acknowledge the worldwide artists whose featured works are above and beyond great works of art. Each hand painted work adds to the beauty of the overall project. The talent that lies within these pages and the pages of the entire series is extraordinary. This art was purchased by the publisher and is Copyright © protected through Fotolia.com and Shutterstock.com.

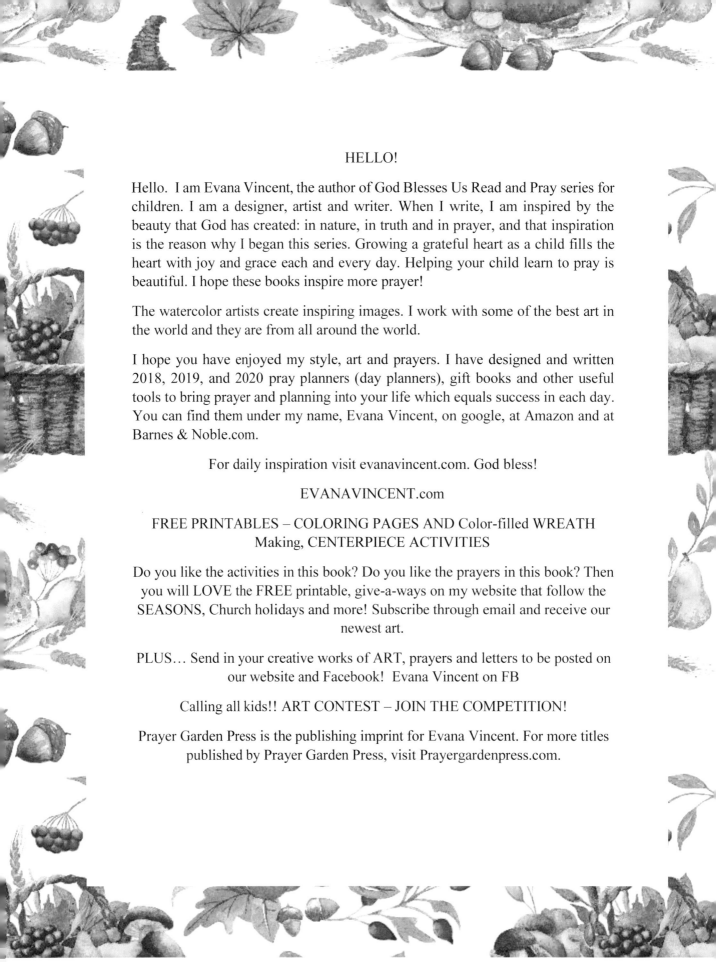

HELLO!

Hello. I am Evana Vincent, the author of God Blesses Us Read and Pray series for children. I am a designer, artist and writer. When I write, I am inspired by the beauty that God has created: in nature, in truth and in prayer, and that inspiration is the reason why I began this series. Growing a grateful heart as a child fills the heart with joy and grace each and every day. Helping your child learn to pray is beautiful. I hope these books inspire more prayer!

The watercolor artists create inspiring images. I work with some of the best art in the world and they are from all around the world.

I hope you have enjoyed my style, art and prayers. I have designed and written 2018, 2019, and 2020 pray planners (day planners), gift books and other useful tools to bring prayer and planning into your life which equals success in each day. You can find them under my name, Evana Vincent, on google, at Amazon and at Barnes & Noble.com.

For daily inspiration visit evanavincent.com. God bless!

EVANAVINCENT.com

FREE PRINTABLES – COLORING PAGES AND Color-filled WREATH Making, CENTERPIECE ACTIVITIES

Do you like the activities in this book? Do you like the prayers in this book? Then you will LOVE the FREE printable, give-a-ways on my website that follow the SEASONS, Church holidays and more! Subscribe through email and receive our newest art.

PLUS… Send in your creative works of ART, prayers and letters to be posted on our website and Facebook! Evana Vincent on FB

Calling all kids!! ART CONTEST – JOIN THE COMPETITION!

Prayer Garden Press is the publishing imprint for Evana Vincent. For more titles published by Prayer Garden Press, visit Prayergardenpress.com.

Made in United States
Troutdale, OR
10/27/2023

14040628R00029